WILDFLOWER

SANVI SONI

ISBN 979-8-89588-942-8

Part 1

Who are you? I don't know.

I wish my words would flow like a symphony.
Or pierce your heart like your favourite song.
Or captivate you like a beautiful painting.
But all I can do is pour my heart,
and spell some words wrong.
But maybe,
between the misspelt words,
scattered thoughts,
and misleading metaphors,
something from my heart will touch yours.
Just maybe.

Never trust my metaphors.

For every way to say I love you,

I have found a way to make it sound not true.

I hide behind my prose

to hide the fact that your words have turned

my cheeks rose.

If I can't let go of the truth

and let it dance with disguise,

maybe the past I will no longer rue

and sometimes I'll let myself love you.

For within my metaphors are exposed naked truths,

hoping to lead you along fallacious paths.

I long for places I've never been to.
I dance to symphonies I cannot hear.
I find myself getting attached to words
I don't know the meanings of.

I don't know a lot of things,
one of which would be myself.
Who am I beneath the sheath of my skin?
Who am I without the syllables I'm called?
Who am I behind the words I speak?

Perhaps, just a thought.
Just a name.
Just someone.
Who wasn't meant to exist,
but does anyway.

Sinking in a corner,
pressed into a wall;
Do they even know I'm present?
Am I here at all?

Is there a written rule book that tells you how to be-
all the right things to talk about-
that everyone has but me?

Slowly, I am withering-
a flower deprived of the sun;
longing to belong somewhere.

I used to capture bugs in jars.
I loved the way they would squirm.
They way they would try climbing the sides,
only to slide back down again.
Sometimes I feel like a helpless bug,
trapped inside a glass jar.
Constantly trying to escape my unfortunate reality,
trying to find a way out.
And just when I think I have found an escape route,
just when I think I have made my way to the opening
of my cruel glass jar.
I slide back down to the bottom,
only to try again tomorrow.

But she tried, she really tried.
To show the world pieces of what life could be.
But bit by bit,
as she gave them pieces of the manic she held dear
like love, golden hour, flowers, art and the stars,
and thing after thing they dismissed telling her-
Love is only infatuation.
Golden hour is only light.
Flowers are only so the plant can make seeds.
Art is only people recreating what's already been.
And stars are just a fire that's far away.
There is nothing magical.

And when their words returned to her,
others' blindness to what she loved
faded her adoration for things
as she slowly started to hate how she saw the world.

Then the girl who once saw the world with colour,
took out her eyes,
because she didn't only see black and white.

From afar, I was the golden child.
Perfect grades, perfect manners.
A trophy for my parents.

Inside, I was slowly dying.
My anxiety was gnawing at my insides at all times.
Being 'good' was the only source of my parents' happiness,
so I strangled my dreams for theirs.

No real friends, no heartbreaks, no parties.
Nothing that will distract me from perfection.

Do they even see me as human?
A human with emotions and feelings?
Or was I just an epitome of control and obedience?

A trophy for my parents.

I often ask myself-

Do I love or do I want proof that I am loveable?

My fist has always been clenched around the handle

of an invisible suitcase.

I am always ready to leave.

There is not a single room in this world where I belong.

I am an observer, but not by choice.

I sit and listen to what people have to say

because I do not have much to say of my own.

I sit and thinly slice their habits and their ways,

I melt their mannerisms and drink the bits I find pleasing,

because comfort in my own skin is something

I have never felt.

No one listened to me.
So I poured a glass,
and got addicted to words.
A drink or two down,
I got intoxicated with rhymes
and drowsy with emotion.

Now, the scent of vodka won't leave me
and poetry spills out of my mouth.
I shattered the glass,
and grabbed a bottle instead;
"Is no one listening?"

Or is it all in my head?

I know exactly who I want to be.

I've shaped this ideal person in my head.

From the colour she paints her nails in winter,

to the silk pyjamas she wears to bed.

I think about her when I mess up,

when things don't go my way.

How she would laugh off the stress,

and know exactly what to say.

She is the version of me that I most want to be.

So happy and kind and always carefree.

I've tried so hard to be this perfect girl,

that I've forgotten how to be me.

I've become an artist.
Whether it's to paint pictures,
or to cut rivers on my body worth drowning in so deep
that I begin to lose myself in them.

It paints this picture,
a picture that is hidden in a confined part of my body
for nobody to see but me.
I am an artist.
A hidden artist.

And yes,
I hate dying,
I hate the hurt,
but at least I'm left with something to feel-
my hidden art.

Sanvi Soni

I pour my soul into these pages,

hoping it would give some release to my head

that has been downing me for ages.

But still, I cannot seem to find my peace.

I just need to feel okay.

But now? I think and think and think.

Maybe it would be easier if someone would stay.

But they all leave in a blink of an eye.

At this point, I don't know what to do.

Like a boat lost in the sea

with no land in sight

I scream for hope, no one's there, just me.

I might just give up on this fight.

The waves would still crash by the shore.

The sun would still rise.

It would be over in a flash.

No one cares about my demise.

I want to live.

I'm just afraid.

I won't measure up to the idea people have of me.

I'm afraid of getting older.

Scared I'll never write anything worth reading again.

That I'll disappoint the people who are counting on me.

That I'll never learn how to be happy.

That I'll be broke one day.

That my parents will die,

and I'll be alone in the end.

What surprises me most about humankind is that
we get bored of our childhood, rush to grow up,
and then long to be children again.
That we lose our health to make money,
and then lose our money to restore our health.
That by thinking anxiously about our future,
we forget the present,
such that we live in neither the present nor the future.
That we live as if we'll never die,
and die as though we've never lived.

Wildflower

She pulls the giant sunflower head to her face,
and counts every seed.
Her tiny fingers graze over them,
as one by one they fall to the grass.
Her laughter tickles my soul.

I'd give anything,
to see that sunflower
through her eyes.
So unfiltered and innocent,
unaware of the weight of the world,
and being altered by its heaviness.

But it won't be beautiful to them,
only us.
We grew up under the same skies.
Played in the same puddles.
Roamed in the same gardens.
And because of this, you'll always know where to find me.
I'll be in the grass watching for shapes in the sky.
Or dancing soaked outside,
as the sound of rain downs out all the voices
saying I'll catch a cold.
Or even though we have a long way to drive,
I'll stop on the road
to pick up lovely weeds.

I know most won't understand.
But you do, because to us
these wonders we hold onto
is what makes the world so beautiful.

Isn't it beautiful,

when someone really knows you?

When they know

why you only like hot coffee, not iced.

Why you cry when you watch La La Land.

Why you hate killing spiders.

Why you love watching documentaries.

Why you love long car rides.

Why your favourite colour is blue.

How lovely it is,

to really be known by someone.

I want to be your favourite book.

I want you to open me up and never let me go.

I want you to read between my lines,

highlight your favourite parts of me.

Inner-stand the language of my soul.

Look into my eyes and discover my previous editions.

Rub your fingertips across the words on my heart.

Decode the chapters of my being.

Study the paragraphs of my mind.

Overstand the meaning of my existence in your world.

Hold me as though you couldn't possibly put me down.

You won't ever need a bookmark,

because you'll never get tired of turning my pages.

I want to be your favourite book.

I love the way you make me feel.
Like a kitchen is for dancing and
that dessert for breakfast is never something to regret.
You've always had this way of making
everything feel like a dream come true.
How lucky I am to be with someone
that holds my heart like a promise they won't break.

We have the kind of love
that people write songs about.
We are the words they can't get out of their head,
and the reason they believe that not all stories have to end.

I hope everyone gets to meet this kind of love.
I hope everyone finds someone,
that makes them believe in forever.

He wasn't my first boyfriend.
He wasn't even my first crush.

But my first love.
He was the boy who looked at me a little too long to be my
friend.
The boy who stayed with me on the playground
when everyone else was gone.
He was the one who was always too close for my boyfriends
to like,
but far enough to ever be one.

The boy who would be my biggest lesson,
because he was the biggest heartbreak.

The boy who I searched for
in everyone else.

We knew of course that our childhood
was nothing more than a glass house.
A wide-eyed wonder that existed to end.

The monkey bar calluses have peeled away.
The scraped knees long since healed.
Do you remember when recklessness was law?
When we could blame our stupidity on our underdeveloped
minds?

Now our faces are in photographs,
and the ink is fading away.
There is a boundlessness buried in the memories
I'm now beginning to forget.
And I fear I'll never reach it,
or you,
ever again.

There will always be a rope between you and me.

When we drifted apart months ago,

we never cut that rope.

We never said goodbye.

We simply called it a 'break',

a pause waiting to be resumed.

It was just that break,

that pause,

which never ended.

The rope which tied us together remained uncut.

In my mind,

you and I,

we will always be connected.

Whether it be a song,

or a place in the depths of lonely nights.

My name will always be at the back of your mind.

And yours will always have a place in my heart.

Just as long as that rope remains uncut.

I want to write you a song.
I hope you'll never know it was written just for you,
but I dream it makes you smile.
Maybe even dance.
A song must be the only way to show how I feel.
But I'm not the one for rhymes and melodies,
so colours on a canvas will just have to do.

Maybe in the way I place the paint
could hold a rhyme,
and the different elements, a melody.
I want my art to be played like your favourite song.
Coming back to it over and over again,
till you've memorised every stroke.
And though you're sick of it,
it's held so dear.

And just as you'll see my soul so generously spilled out,
you'll find fractions of your own.

Part 2

I love you, I'm sorry.

Wildflower

I'm losing you.
We don't talk the way we used to.
I kept thinking about what went wrong between us.
But the answer is nothing is wrong,
you never truly wanted me.

Accepting the truth hurts the most.
Sadly, you made me think that you've fallen for me too.
I thought you were my 'right place, right time'.
I really thought I meant something to you.

I would do anything to make you stay,
because the thought of you being with someone else
it scares me to death.

I loved you,
what happened?

Right now,

I think I would give up a future love story of mine

just to relive ours.

You told me to find someone new

but my idiotic heart couldn't move on from you.

I'm still the same as I always was.

Still at the shore

watching the waves crash against the sand,

knowing what I feel for you

cannot be conveyed in phrasal combinations.

It screams out loud,

or stays painfully silent.

But I promise you,

it beats words,

It beats worlds.

To him,
she was just some girl.
But to her,
oh wow.

She saw every one of his flaws
and turned them into perfections.
She had pictured them together
a million times.
She cried until there was nothing left
unable to breathe over this boy.

He wasn't just another boy to her.
She would walk to the ends of the world for him,
but he wouldn't walk two feet for her.

More than friends, less than lovers.

Walking the fine line between falling in love and breaking hearts.

Never too many compliments, or too many people knowing.

One person wanting to give their all,

and the other wanting to pull back.

It starts exciting, and thrilling

but slowly fades into difficult, and complicated.

More than friends, less than lovers.

No one saying how they feel, for fear it will be over.

Knowing everything and another about the other.

Little pieces of them, etching into your soul.

Until one day, it's just not enough.

You are not enough.

More than friends, less than lovers.

I begged the stars for more time with you,
and yet they took you away.
They left me guessing where you could have gone.
They left me wondering which star is you.
I wonder why they heard my cries and took you away.
I wonder why they saw my tears and took you away.

I wonder why they chose you.

It's like when you finish a really good book.
Along the way, you find yourself
invested in the lives of the characters,
you fall in love with their voice,
you're attached to the storyline.
You want nothing but one more chapter.

But now that book is finished.
And I can't bring myself to pick a new one.
I don't want something different.
My mind is still stuck on this story.
My mind is still stuck on our story.

I remember those days with you,
when I was the happiest.
My smile reached to my ears,
and my heart was living on cloud nine.
There was something about the way your hands
fit perfectly into my back pockets.
The way you brought me back to earth.

I still believe that you and I were made for each other.
But as the days pass by like a slow-moving train,
I've learned to accept that forever wasn't meant for us in this life.
But I hope in the next one,
we will know how to get it right.

I'm learning to rewrite love
without mentioning your name.
So far,
the page is blank.

You are the only thing about love I have ever known.

A name, that's all that it is.
7 letters.
But suddenly those 7 letters spell out an eternity of
stories, promises, and memories,
that sometimes I wish I could forget.

A name, that's all that it is.
But I've scribbled it across this page over a thousand times,
as if you might materialize if I write it down enough.
I'm still trying to accept the fact that
crossing P's and A's won't bring people back.

So, when they see it in the margins and ask what I've written
down.
And when they see me flinch when I hear it out loud.
I swallow those 7 letters,
and say,
'A name, that's all that it is."

Your favourite song came on in the car yesterday.

And god,

for those 3 minutes and 26 seconds,

I let myself believe that you were still in my life.

I would give anything
to go back to when it all started.
Waking on in your sweater and holding your hand.
When we didn't need coffee to keep us awake,
because the beginning of our love made us feel alive.
You were my favourite good morning
and my most beautiful goodnight.
But it really was the in-between
that felt like a dream come true.

The days were never long enough for our kind of love.
I wish it was the first day of summer again
when it wasn't too late and our hearts were right on time.

We were like a book that I didn't want to put down.
But I'm still trying to forget the chapter
where you broke us in half because
I only want to remember the part
where being with you felt like a sunrise.

I hope one day I'll find a way to stop writing
my story like you're still a part of it.

If I ever see a flaw of yours,
I'd say my eyes are the flawed ones.

"It's okay."
She whispered to herself.
"It's okay."
But is it?

She gave everything she had to others.
She carved her soul for the people around her.
But now,
when she needs the same,
She has no one to turn to.
No one will rescue her the way she rescued them.

So she sits on the floor
telling herself,
"It's okay."
Knowing it's not.
Knowing it never will be.

No one's perfect, but I thought we were.
We fit so well together.
But what if I was just imagining this?
Looking over our flaws like they didn't exist,
Pretending everything was fine between us.
It hurt to much to think otherwise,
so I just imagined we were.

If we were perfect
my heart wouldn't have been broken.
If we were perfect
I wouldn't be crying every time I caught myself alone.
If we were perfect
It wouldn't have ended.

Wildflower

When our garden was devastated
by a fire you started,
you ran to someone else.
You started growing something new.
While I was left there all alone,
feeling nothing but betrayed, abandoned, worthless.

I didn't move on.
I stayed there for a while
and laid in the ashes of our so-called 'love'.
A place I used to feel safe in,
a place I used to call my home.

Finally, I walked away with the ash and seeds in my hair.
I hoped to sprout roots in my skull,
a garden in my mind no one could ever devastate again.
For once, I knew,
all the love I had was mine.

I killed myself that day.
There was no funeral, no flowers on my grave.
My friends did not create rivers from salty tears,
and they did not pray to the gods they believed in
for me to come back.
I killed that version of me,
the one I was with you.
I left her in the burning house.
The one you set on fire before you walked away.
I probably could have followed you out the door,
tried to escape the fumes of smoke.

But I didn't.
I couldn't.
I let that version of me die that day.

I was burning
while you came blaming me for the smell of ashes.

It's a different kind of grief
when the person you miss is still alive.
When they are just a phone call away.
When you can still text them in the morning
and before you go to sleep at night.
When you can walk 15 minutes to your favourite
coffee shop and meet at the park bench for lunch.

Isn't it torture?
This choice to keep missing them
and holding hope that maybe,
just maybe,
they miss you too.

Part 3

Sad birds still sing.

Wildflower

You loved me like a flower,

the ones you leave out to die.

Instead of loving me like the wild,

you kept me locked inside.

You let me slowly wild

until there was only a piece of who I was.

Keeping something wild, untamed, undisturbed,

locked inside the same four walls,

you should see what it does.

How it turns life into a greyscaled canvas

with having nothing to look forward to.

It feels as if you're stuck in this endless loop of nothingness

with no escape, no way out.

So, if you ever meet a girl like me,

I ask you to let her blossom,

let her live,

let her go.

Then you can see what happens,

when you let a wildflower grow.

The age-old question:
"Is it better to have loved and lost
or to never have loved at all?"

But darling,
I'd lose you a million times over
if it meant that I could love you just once more.

I wrote a poem about it
and then I threw it away
because that's the last thing I need right now.

More words dedicated to someone,
that never dedicated a single thing to me.

Sometimes I scared
I'll never fall in love again.
I don't feel too comfortable.
I lose interest quickly.
I don't get too involved.

But I realised it's not true,
I fall in love every day.

With all these pink and purple sunsets.
With the fearless laugh of my friends.
With the beginning of a new book.
With the time I share with my parents.
With the emotion when I hug my sister.
With the music that makes me dance.
With the inevitable enthusiasm of travelling.
With the vivid smell and sound of the ocean.
With the sun burning against my skin on a summer day.

I fall in love every day,
just not in a romantic way.

I blinked, and everything was over.

I blinked, and I grew up.

Nothing was the same.

My world had changed and I didn't even notice.

I blinked, and that was it.

I was no longer the little girl getting on the school bus.

I was no longer the little girl who cried in her dad's arms.

I was no longer a little girl.

I blinked and reality struck me

and knocked me down.

I blinked and now I grieved for that little girl.

The scared, sad, little girl I was.

I grew up and didn't know until it was too late.

I know it's hard.

Believe me.

I know what it feels like.

Tomorrow will never come

and today will be the most difficult day to get through.

But I swear you will get through.

The hurt will pass,

as it always does.

If you give it time and let it go,

it will move slowly.

Like a broken promise,

let it go.

Wildflower

She walks alone in the rain

letting the drops of water run down her face,

mixing with the salty tears

she desperately tries to hold in.

But as those tears are joined with the rain,

she feels safe to let them out.

It puts her at ease,

it's almost like she isn't alone anymore.

So, she continues on.

Letting the world melt around her,

giving her a cold, bitter hug

reminding her that life isn't so lonely after all.

Maybe, just maybe
in another universe
there is a little girl
with long, black hair
and she is loved right
by the people that who were supposed to love her.

She lays in fields of flowers
as butterflies dance on her cheeks,
and the burn from the sun
is the most painful thing
she ever feels.

Sometimes when I laugh
I sound just like my mom.
And sometimes when I look in the mirror,
I see my dad looking back at me.
One day, my mom and dad will be gone.
That's the way it's supposed to be.
I don't want to live without them,
but even more,
I don't want to force them to live without me.

So, when I'm seventy-two
and the earth is dying
and my parents will be gone,
all I hope is that my laugh is still my mom's
and my face is still my dad's.

Three minutes until I'm a year closer to whatever is meant to be.
Or maybe we don't know what's meant to be until we die.
Till our bodies decompose in the dirt
and grow flowers over our graves.
Maybe that's the time we realise that
birthdays are significant.
No matter how hard you try to forget
the year is gone but you still have you.

It's a beautiful thing
not to have lost yourself.
But such a woeful thing
to be reminded
that you still have time to lose yourself.

Wildflower

For the first time in my life
I woke up without a knife in my chest,
and an empty heart at best.
I woke up without the condescending thoughts
of having to live another day.

For the first time in my life
I wanted to be awake.
I wanted to be able to watch my friends grow,
and go to whatever shows I want.
For the first time in my life
I felt like I'd found someone,
someone who not only understand
but withstands who I am.
For the first time in my life,
I woke up with my cup not half full or half empty.
I woke up with a cup with more than plenty.

I realised,
I'm no longer stuck;
waking up only to wish I could just go back to sleep.
Now I sit and see,
how beautiful relationships can be
if they are right.

My sunshine was stolen from me when I was fourteen.

When my siblings looked to me as their parent.
When the loss was too grave to comprehend.
When the nights were too loud, and the days were too silent.
When I was looked at as an outcast, yet leaned upon like a pillar.

I searched my sunshine in every love,
in every therapy session,
in every friendship,
in every tiny connection.

In every place where I believed my sunshine to be.
Until I searched within the place I thought it was stolen.

And realised,
the sunshine was me.

Some of us are glass,

we shatter when we are dropped.

Some of us are paper,

we tear when we are pulled.

Some of us are rocks,

we split when we are forced.

But some of us are stones in an ocean,

we don't have a specific cause for our wear.

We are not shattered, not torn, or split

but we are damaged just as much.

You don't always need a reason.

I stopped waiting for that train that may never come.
That ship that may never sail.
That bus that may never pull up to my stop.
That text that may never be sent.
That call that may never be dialled.
Or those words I wanted to hear come out of your mouth.

I stopped waiting.
I stopped waiting.

I stopped waiting for you to make my vision of us real.
For you to complete my world.
For you to be my happily ever after.
I stopped waiting.
I stopped waiting.

I stopped waiting for you
because maybe
someone may be waiting for me.

It hits you
in the middle of doing your grocery shopping with your mother,
when you're chatting with an old friend,
doing the laundry,
cleaning your room,
laughing at a funny video,
or singing along in the car.

When you think you've healed.
When you aren't thinking about it.

Life moves on.
The clock ticks,
and it hits you all over again.
Acknowledge it.
Feel it.
Then let it pass,
because it will
and it always does.

I saw her sitting there.
A younger, smaller version of me.
At fourteen years old, sitting on my childhood bed.
I slowly walked to her and knelt,
I took her hands in mine.
She looked up at me,
and with a small voice asked
"Does it get any better?".

I squeezed her hands,
"No, not for a long time. It doesn't get better for a long time."
She closed her eyes and tears
streamed down her face.
I let go of her hands
and placed mine around her small face.
"Does anyone end up saving us?" she softly asked.

I smiled,
"Yes," I said.
She then looked up at me, hopeful.
"Who saves us?"

"We do, we save ourselves."

The bees aren't going away,
but they will change with you.
Sometimes they will be chaotic,
sometimes they will give you sweet honey,
and sometimes they will remind you
of how much love can sting.

But if you find a home within yourself,
and make peace with your bees,
you will be alright.